Seward's Folly

CORNERSTONES OF FREEDOM™

SECOND SERIES

Melissa Whitcraft

Children's Press®
A Division of Scholastic Inc.
New York • Toronto • London • Auckland • Sydney
Mexico City • New Delhi • Hong Kong
Danbury, Connecticut

Photographs © 2002: Alaska State Library: 21, 28 right (Alaska Purchase Centennial Collection), 24, 44 right (Willis T. Geisman/U.S. Office of the Territories), 28 left, 29; Anchorage Museum of History and Art: 8 (AT 1-8); Archive Photos/Getty Images/New York Times Co.: 33 top; Brown Brothers: 10, 19; Corbis Images: 20 right, 32 (Bettmann), 5 top (Jack Fields), 18 (Museum of History and Industry), 39 (Yogi, Inc.), cover top, 22, 25; Dembinsky Photo Assoc./Rob Starleton: 38, 45 top right; Folio, Inc./Rob Crandall: 35; Hulton Archive/Getty Images: 17; Library of Congress: cover bottom; Network Aspen/Ricardo Savi: 41; North Wind Picture Archives: 11, 44 left; Peter Arnold Inc.: 23, 26 (Clyde H. Smith), 9 (James G. Wark); Photo Researchers, NY: 7 (Michael Giannechini), 40 (Ted Kerasote); Stock Montage, Inc.: 3 background, 4, 15; Stone/Getty Images/Art Wolfe: 6; Superstock, Inc.: 33 bottom, 45 top left (Ernest Manewal), 34 (John W. Warden), 12, 13; The Image Works/Topham: 20 left; University of Alaska, Fairbanks/William Egan/Elmer E. Rasmuson Library: 30, 31, 45 bottom; Visuals Unlimited: 5 bottom (Gerald & Buff Corsi), 36 (Patrick Endres).

Library of Congress Cataloging-in-Publication Data

Whitcraft, Melissa.
    Seward's folly / Melissa Whitcraft.
      p. cm. — (Cornerstones of freedom. Second series)
    Summary: Explores the history of Alaska, its path to statehood, and current issues, including the conflict between those who want to drill for oil in new locations and those who wish to protect the environment. Includes bibliographical references and index.
    ISBN 0-516-22525-1
    1. Alaska—History—Juvenile literature. [1. Alaska—History.] I. Title. II. Series.
  F904.3 .W48 2002
  979.8—dc21

                                              2002001647

1 2 3 4 5 6 7 8 9 10 R 11 10 09 08 07 06 05 04 03 02

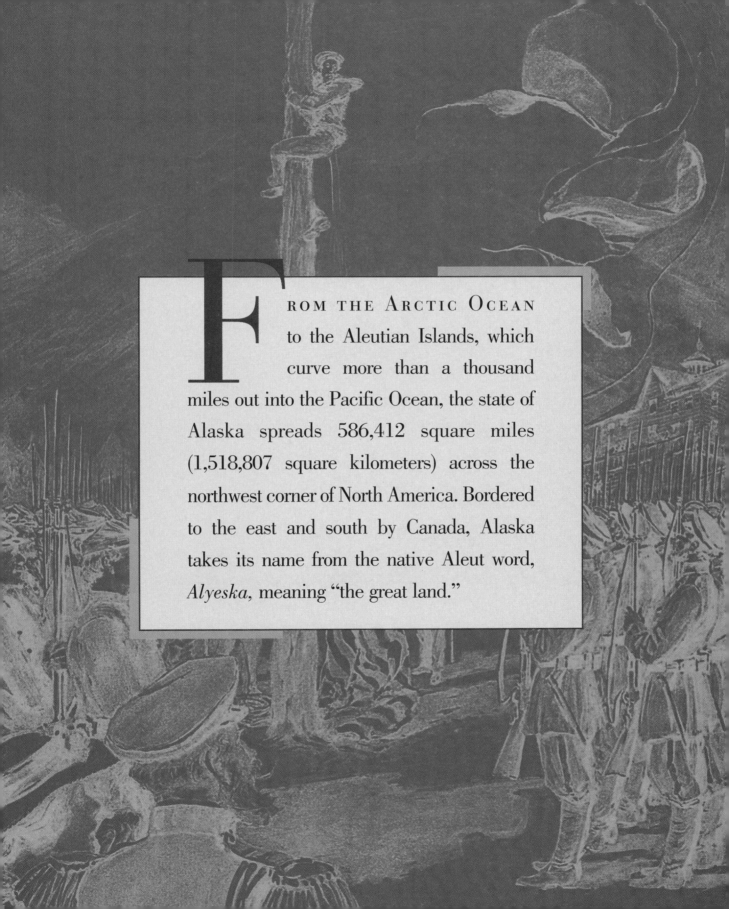

ROM THE ARCTIC OCEAN
to the Aleutian Islands, which
curve more than a thousand
miles out into the Pacific Ocean, the state of
Alaska spreads 586,412 square miles
(1,518,807 square kilometers) across the
northwest corner of North America. Bordered
to the east and south by Canada, Alaska
takes its name from the native Aleut word,
Alyeska, meaning "the great land."

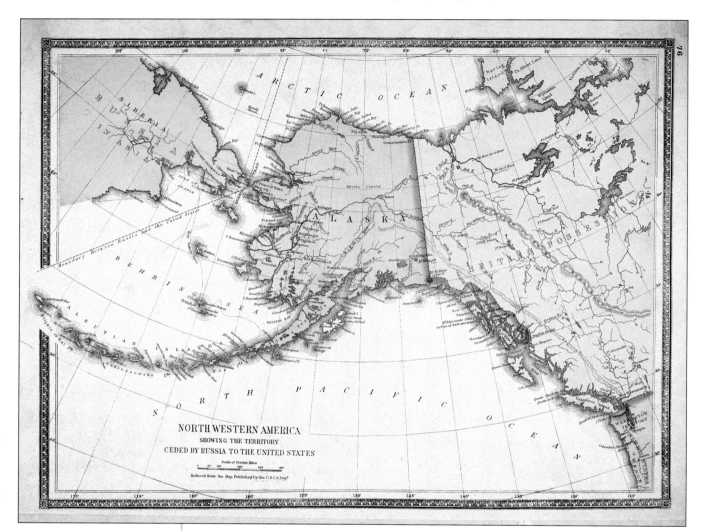

NORTH WESTERN AMERICA
SHOWING THE TERRITORY
CEDED BY RUSSIA TO THE UNITED STATES

Scale of Statute Miles

Reduced from the Map Published by the U.S.C.S. Dep.t

The state of Alaska sits between the countries of Russia and Canada.

Rich in **natural resources,** the state is indeed a great land. Its oil, fishing, timber, and mining industries produce millions of dollars in **revenue** yearly. In addition, every year more than a million tourists come from all over the world to experience the magnificent beauty of Alaska's ancient mountains, forests, glaciers, rivers, and ragged coastlines. Today, Alaska thrives, and its importance as a state is obvious.

Oil and timber are two
major industries found
in Alaska.

★ ★ ★ ★

ALASKA'S MAJESTY

Alaska's natural beauty includes 33,904 miles (54,563 kilometers) of shoreline, three million lakes, three thousand rivers, and the country's sixteen highest mountains. In addition to 430 different species of birds, Alaskan wildlife includes bear, moose, sheep, and caribou, but no reptiles.

Mount McKinley, Alaska's most famous mountain

Riley Creek, which flows
below Mount Healy in the
background

It was not always so. For years—many Alaskans believe
for too many years—the country's largest state was a joke to
Americans living in the **Lower 48.** The territory was seen
as a huge, useless "icebox," the **folly** of a man who didn't
know what he was doing. Over time, however, people's
opinion changed. The story of this change is the story of
Alaska's long journey to statehood.

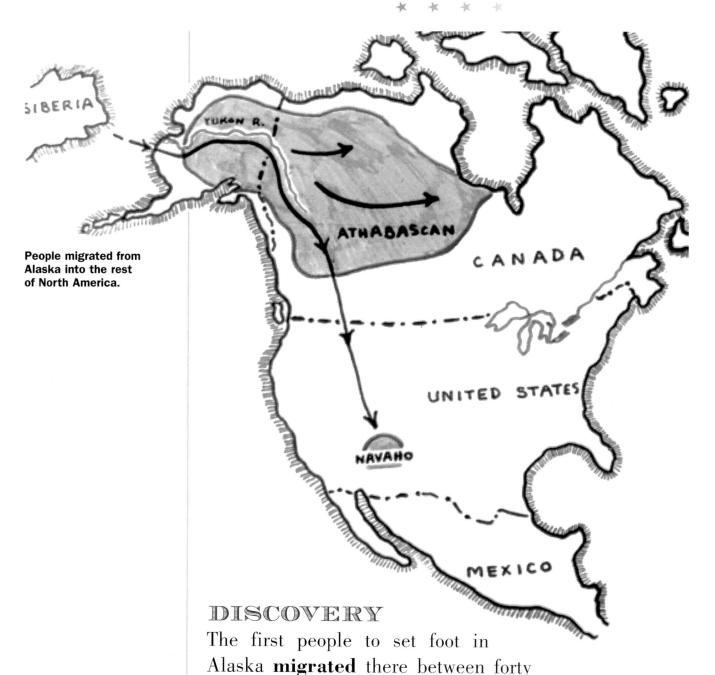

People migrated from Alaska into the rest of North America.

SIBERIA

YUKON R.

ATHABASCAN

CANADA

UNITED STATES

NAVAHO

MEXICO

DISCOVERY

The first people to set foot in
Alaska **migrated** there between forty
thousand and fourteen thousand years ago.
They crossed the land bridge that connected what is now
Russia to North America. Following animal trails, many of
these early hunters continued south into the Pacific

Northwest. The ones who remained and settled mostly along the Alaskan coast evolved into such diverse native civilizations as the Tlingit, Haida, Athabascons, Aleuts, Yupiks, Gwich'in, and Inupiaq.

Around ten thousand years ago, melting glaciers from the Ice Age flooded the land bridge. Alaska had no further contact with Europeans until the Russians arrived in 1741.

Malaspina Glacier

ALASKA'S GLACIERS

Alaska is still covered by almost 20,000 miles (32,000 km) of glaciers. Malaspina Glacier, the largest in North America, is 850 miles (1,360 km) long.

At that time, Vitus Bering, a Dane sailing with the Russian navy, landed on Kayak Island. Bering's arrival by ship proved that Russia and North America were not connected as many people had thought. A sea that now bears Bering's name separated the two landmasses.

For the next 126 years the Russians colonized Alaska. They developed a booming fur trade, sent Christian missionaries, and enslaved the Aleuts. In 1804 they built a capital, which is now called Sitka. By 1867 profits from the fur trade had dropped so low that Russia was no longer interested in maintaining its colony. Alaska, once so promising, had become a burden.

Vitus Bering, after whom the Bering Sea and Bering Strait are named.

SEWARD'S DREAM

To William Henry Seward, President Andrew Johnson's secretary of state, Alaska was not a burden. It was an opportunity. Seward wanted the United States to become a world power. He believed, therefore, that the country had to expand its territory as far as possible. He started planning for this expansion as early as 1852 when he was a senator from New York. At that time he asked for a naval survey of

William Henry Seward

both the Bering Strait and the north Pacific. A year later, further defending his position, Seward said he hoped that someday the "federal republic . . . shall be extended so that it shall greet the sun when he touches the tropics and when he sends his gleaming rays towards the polar circle."

WILLIAM HENRY SEWARD (1801–1872)

Seward was a creative public servant throughout his life. It was his belief that in addition to territorial expansion, the transcontinental railroad and telegraph, as well as liberal immigration policies and naturalization laws, would help make the United States a world power.

Buying Alaska, therefore, was the perfect step to take to insure America's future. The country had already expanded westward. California became a state in 1850. If Seward could get the government to agree to buy Russia's colony, it would increase the country's chances of becoming, as Seward hoped, the "Power of the Pacific Ocean."

Getting Congress to agree to the purchase, however, would not be easy. In 1867 the country was still recovering from the Civil War, which had ended in 1865. Buying and settling a new territory thousands of miles away was not a high priority. Even though Seward had also been President Lincoln's secretary of state, many Americans, in and out of government, distrusted Andrew Johnson, who became president after Lincoln was assassinated.

To keep Congress out of the initial discussions, Seward negotiated with the Russians in secret. Then on the night of March 30, 1867, he signed the treaty agreeing to buy Alaska for $7.2 million, or approximately 2 cents an acre.

William H. Seward signs the Alaska Purchase Treaty with the Russians on March 30, 1867. Shown here are (from left to right) Robert S. Chew, Seward, William Hunter, Mr. Bodisco, Baron de Stolckl, Charles Sumner, and Frederick W. Seward.

SEWARD'S FOLLY

Once he had the signed treaty, Seward went to work to convince Congress to accept it. He asked Civil War heroes to write supportive letters. He had sympathetic newspapers write favorable articles. *The New York Times,* for example, printed a bold headline that read "BRIGHT PROSPECTS FOR OUR JAPAN AND CHINA TRADE." Seward also asked those congressmen who agreed with the purchase to defend the treaty to those who opposed it.

These congressional supporters argued in favor of the purchase because it would give the country a naval base on the Pacific. It also would provide safe harbors for American trading ships and might even convince Canada, which bordered the territory, to break with England and join the United States.

Those who opposed the treaty also had plenty to say. Newspapers such as the *Daily Gazette* in Cincinnati said that Seward had only signed it to keep the country from realizing what a terrible job he and President Johnson were doing on the home front.

In Congress, opponents thought $7.2 million was too much to pay. Others did not support Seward's dreams for expansion. Many believed it was more important to spend the time and money on rebuilding the nation's **economy**, which had suffered terribly during the Civil War.

After a long delay and much debate, Congress finally agreed to accept the treaty. Seward's point of view won over some congressmen, who accepted the need to develop a Pacific trade. Others supported the treaty

The American flag is raised in Alaska on October 18, 1867, marking the transfer of Alaska from Russian to American control.

because Russia had helped the Union during the Civil War, and they felt that this was a good way to repay the Russians. On October 18, at a ceremony on the barren Alaskan coast, Russian and American cannons were fired. The Russian flag was lowered, and the American flag was raised.

Even after the fact, most Americans thought the purchase was ridiculous. Alaska—or "Walrussia," as some mockingly called the new territory—was too cold, too huge, and too far away to be useful to the country. Alaska was a joke. It became known as Seward's Folly. But Seward truly believed that Alaska, "first as a territory, and ultimately as a state or many states, [would] prove . . . worthy as an addition to the United States."

THE NEW TERRITORY

The new territory had to be governed. Peace had to be maintained between the white settlers and the **indigenous** tribes, who were worried about losing their land. President Johnson chose the navy to do the job because most settlements hugged Alaska's southeastern **panhandle** coast and were easily reachable by boat.

Alaska didn't get a civil, or nonmilitary, government until 1884, when Congress passed the First Organic Act. This act, or law, gave the territory laws, judges, and sheriffs. It did not, however, address the question of rights for the more than thirty thousand native people of Alaska. Nor did it mention the possibility of statehood.

★ ★ ★ ★

Klondike gold miners. Alaska's population grew as prospectors moved to the Klondike in search of gold.

Nevertheless, because it gave the territory a set of civilian laws that connected it directly to the federal government in Washington, D.C., the act was Alaska's first small step toward statehood.

GOLD!

A more important step was the discovery of gold at the Klondike River in the Yukon Territory of Canada in 1896. The following summer, **prospectors** sailing out of Alaskan ports returned to Seattle, Washington, and excitedly threw gold **nuggets** onto the docks. The message was clear. There was gold to spare!

★ ★ ★ ★

To get to the Klondike, prospectors, or "stampeders" as they were called, had to pass through Alaska. One of the more famous and dangerous routes cut over the mountains at the Chilkoot Pass. In the winter this pass, which rose 1,000 feet (30.5 meters) in the last half-mile, became known as the "golden staircase."

Consisting of 15,000 steps carved out of ice, the "staircase" made it possible for determined prospectors to get across the mountains. The journey, however, was terrifying. Carrying 50- to 60-pound (22.5-27 kilogram) packs on their backs, these men, and some women, had to climb, single-file, through freezing temperatures and biting blizzards. Few turned back. Similar to those who returned to Seattle, many believed that they too would have enough good luck to throw gold nuggets away.

People with sled dogs head up the "golden staircase" of Chilkoot Pass.

Nome, Alaska, 1898,
already fairly well populated

All of these people searching for gold changed Alaska. Before the rush, the few hundred white settlers who came did so for fur trading, fishing, and seal hunting. Once the search moved beyond the Klondike, thousands of people poured into Alaska to look for gold in its rivers, hills, mountains, and beaches. Those not looking for gold came hoping they would make their fortune off the towns that were springing up all over the territory.

When gold was discovered on the beach off the Bering Sea, for example, the population of the small settlement of Nome exploded. By 1900 over twenty thousand people lived in this tiny, isolated village. As in other mining communities, conditions were terrible. In warm weather, the streets, thick with mud, were impassable. Housing was poor and many people lived in tents. Worse, there was no civil order.

19

Still, drawn by the gold, people came. Realizing the crisis, President William McKinley asked Congress to pass more civil and criminal laws for Alaska. He also appointed more judges and started a railroad to connect the port of Seward with the interior town of Fairbanks.

THE KENNECOTT COPPER MINE

Now a tourist site, the Kennecott mine was one of the Alaska Syndicate's more successful operations. Between 1911 and 1938, it produced 591,535 tons (536,632 metric tons) of copper and 562,500 pounds (255,146 kilograms) of silver valued at a combined total of $287 million.

A NEW APPRECIATION

Alaska was no longer a useless icebox. Businesspeople from around the country began to see its potential. Two of the more famous were J.P. Morgan and Daniel Guggenheim. They founded the Alaska Syndicate, which controlled Alaskan salmon **canneries.** It also owned trading companies, mines, railroads, and two steamship corporations. Morgan and

J.P. Morgan and Daniel Guggenheim, founders of the Alaska Syndicate

Alaskan statehood advocate James Wickersham

Guggenheim were making so much money from Alaska's natural resources that editorials in Alaskan newspapers described them as greedy villains who cared nothing for the territory that made them wealthy.

If Morgan and Guggenheim were villains to Alaskans, James Wickersham was a hero. President McKinley appointed him an Alaskan district judge in 1900. From that time until his death in 1939, Wickersham never stopped working for Alaska. In 1908 he became Alaska's **delegate** to Congress. Wickersham could not vote, but as Alaska's

**Chief of Forestry
Gifford Pinchot**

representative, or voice, in Washington, D.C., he was allowed to speak. And speak he did. In 1916 he was the first person to introduce a bill asking for Alaskan statehood.

THE SECOND ORGANIC ACT

While Wickersham continually demanded rights for Alaska, the territory's need for protection was also brought to light by the Ballinger-Pinchot affair. In 1910, Gifford Pinchot, the Chief of Forestry, discovered that the Secretary of the Interior, Richard Ballinger, had illegally transferred thirty-three federal coal land claims over to Daniel Guggenheim. In response, the government called for a congressional investigation, which led to the Second Organic Act of 1912.

This act gave Alaskans the right to elect a local **legislature,** consisting of eight senators and sixteen House members. Laws governing Alaska were now written in Alaska, not Washington, D.C., but the federal government still appointed the territory's governor. Since this governor had the right to veto, or reject, any laws the local legislature passed, Alaska still had no real power to govern itself.

Consequently, Alaska struggled throughout the 1920s and 1930s. Its **infrastructure** was improved when the railroad between Seward and Fairbanks was completed

* * * *

Seaplanes at port in Lake Hood

ALASKA'S RELIANCE ON AIRPLANES

Because of Alaska's mountainous terrain and huge size, airplanes are its major form of transportation. Lake Hood in Anchorage is the world's largest and most active seaplane port. In 1996 one out of every fifty-eight Alaskans had a pilot's license.

and when small airplane services began to connect remote communities to larger towns. However, businesses continued to pocket millions of dollars from Alaska's resources, and the federal government did little to stop this economic drain.

Then came the Depression. All over the United States banks closed, farms failed, and businesses went under. People lost their jobs, their homes, and their savings. Alaska, too, suffered in this financial disaster that affected most of the world. The price of copper went down, as did the price

A farmer holds his crop in the Matanuska-Susitna Valley.

of fish. Between 1929 and 1932, more than half the work-force was unemployed. Those who continued to work did so for less pay.

In 1935 the federal government came up with a plan to boost Alaska's economy. Two hundred farm families from the Lower 48 were given the chance to start over in the Matanuska-Susitna Valley. The Matanuska-Susitna Valley covers 23,000 square miles (59,600 square kilometers) of south central Alaska. It is excellent farmland because winds that blow into the valley from glacier-covered mountains continually deposit fresh, mineral-rich glacial silt onto the land. This silt, which is like fine sand, keeps the soil fertile.

WAR

If the Depression strengthened the relationship between the United States and Alaska, World War II cemented it. On December 7, 1941, when the Japanese attacked the American naval base at Pearl Harbor, Hawaii, President Franklin D. Roosevelt declared war on Japan. The United States entered the Second World War, and Alaska's location became very important.

Japanese attack Dutch Harbor, June 3, 1942.

25

Dutch Harbor, Unalaska Peninsula, part of the Aleutian Islands that curve out into the Pacific

In 1867, Seward imagined that Alaska would become a stepping stone to further American trade in the Pacific. Now the territory was seen as a defensive outpost to protect the country from its enemy. After all, the northernmost Japanese naval base came within 750 miles (1,200 km) of the Aleutian Islands.

26

* * * *

How real the threat was became clear on June 3, 1942, when the Japanese invaded the Aleutians. This attack was the only invasion of the United States in World War II. In 1943 the American army drove the Japanese out and fortified the islands against future invasion. In addition, military bases were established all over Alaska, and the 1,500-mile (2,400 km) Alaska-Canada (Alcan) Highway, which was started in 1942, was completed. Today, this highway, which was constructed to transport military supplies, is the main overland route between Alaska and the rest of North America.

The expanded military presence during World War II increased Alaska's population. In 1940 there were approximately 1,000 military people in the territory. By 1943 that number had risen to 152,000. After the war ended in 1945, some military personnel left. Many, however, remained, and Alaska's importance as a defense base continued because of the Cold War between the United States and what was then the **communist** Soviet Union.

THE "LOOTED LAND"

By the early 1950s, Alaskans were more determined than ever to demand statehood. With outside companies continuing to control its economy, Alaska had no tax money to build roads, hospitals, and schools. There were no laws to regulate shipping or fishing. No one listened to the concerns of the native population. As an article in the national magazine *Newsweek* said, Alaska was a "looted land."

THE COLD WAR

The Cold War refers to the political tension that existed between the United States and communist nations controlled by what is now Russia. This friction influenced American foreign policy from the end of World War II until the end of the 1980s.

Edward Lewis "Bob" Bartlett and Ernest Gruening both fought for Alaska's statehood.

Many people realized that the looting of Alaska's natural resources would only come under control when Alaska became a state. Alaska had to have a locally elected governor and voting representatives in Congress for its voice to be heard over the voices of those more concerned with profits than Alaska's well-being.

Two men in particular recognized that only statehood would save Alaska. One, Edward Lewis "Bob" Bartlett, was appointed secretary of Alaska in 1939 by President Roosevelt. In 1944 he was appointed the territorial delegate to Congress. Like Wickersham before him, Bartlett often spoke about Alaska's rights. In 1948 he introduced his own bill for statehood. The bill did not pass, but when Alaska finally achieved statehood in 1959, Bartlett was elected senator and served until his death in 1968.

The other man who fought for Alaska's statehood was Ernest Gruening. Raised on the East Coast, Gruening also came to Alaska in 1939 when President Roosevelt made him governor of the territory. Well-known in Washington, D.C., Gruening put together a "Committee of One Hundred" in 1949. The committee's purpose was to lobby, or influence, the Congress to make Alaska a state. Eleanor Roosevelt, President Roosevelt's widow, was a vocal member of the

Elizabeth Wanamaker Peratrovich

ELIZABETH WANAMAKER PERATROVICH (1911–1958)

If Bartlett and Gruening were champions for statehood, Peratrovich, a Tlinget, was a champion for Native Alaskan rights. Among other accomplishments, in 1945, she convinced the Alaskan Legislature to pass the Anti-Discrimination Act. This law gave Native Alaskans equal access to public places.

Alaskan Constitutional Convention

committee, as were the famous movie star James Cagney and the author Pearl S. Buck. With the help of these influential Americans and others as well, Gruening kept the issue of Alaskan statehood alive. However, when the Korean War broke out in 1950, Congress turned its focus to winning this new war in Asia.

"WE DEMAND EQUALITY"

Once the war ended in 1953, Alaskans began their push for statehood again. Tired of waiting for the politicians in Congress to act, they decided to write their state constitution, or collection of laws, without the federal government's go-ahead. On April 11, 1955, they held the Alaskan Constitutional Convention in Fairbanks. At that convention Ernest Gruening delivered a powerful speech titled "Let Us Now End American Colonialism."

In his address Gruening described how unfairly the federal government treated Alaska. It was so bad that it reminded Gruening of how the British had treated its American colonies before the American Revolution. He said the treatment was "no less [a] tyranny in 1955 than it was in 1775." Using the fishing industry as one of many examples, Gruening stated that "the federal government had totally ignored . . . the petitions, pleas, [and] prayers . . . of the whole Alaskan people for measures that would conserve that resource."

Describing those who had come to Alaska, Gruening said that they had come "from the forty-eight states, following the most cherished American trend, the westward march in search of greater freedom and greater opportunity." One can hear Seward's voice, Seward's dream for Alaska's future, in Gruening's words.

Finally, Gruening pleaded for statehood, saying, "We Alaskans believe passionately that American citizenship is the most precious possession in the world. Hence we want it in full measure; full citizenship instead of half-citizenship. . . . We demand equality with all other Americans, and the liberties, long denied us, that go with it."

Gruening's pleas were forceful, but Alaska's fight for statehood was not over. As the *Washington Post* newspaper described it, the "murky cloud of politics" still hung over the issue. In Congress, Democrats and Republicans were fighting over which party would control the government. Republicans,

President Dwight D. Eisenhower signs the bill making Alaska a state.

* * * *

including President Eisenhower, initially blocked Alaska's bid for statehood because they felt its citizens would elect Democratic representatives. Republicans believed they would lose their political edge if that happened.

Despite this "cloud," the drive for statehood kept moving forward. One important influence on public opinion was the novel *Ice Palace*. Written in 1958 by the American author Edna Ferber, *Ice Palace* described the bitter battle between those who wanted to keep Alaska a territory and those who wanted the territory to become a state. Gruening, who spoke with Ferber often when she was writing the book, was convinced the novel helped the public understand the importance of Alaskan statehood. As he wrote to Ferber, "Whenever people [talk] about Alaska. . . they [talk] about *Ice Palace*, and they [have] gotten the message."

In addition, Gruening and Bartlett kept up the pressure in Washington. They continued to sway the opinions of hesitant congressmen until Congress voted in favor of statehood. The long struggle was

Edna Ferber, author of *Ice Palace*

ALASKA GETS A FLAG

Alaska's flag was designed in 1926 by thirteen-year-old Native Alaskan Bennie Benson. It consisted of the Big Dipper and the North Star on a blue background. The blue symbolizes the Alaskan sky; the Big Dipper, or Great Bear, its strength; the North Star, the future.

The Alaskan state flag

finally over. On January 3, 1959, almost ninety-two years after Seward signed the treaty with the Russians, President Eisenhower signed the official document making Alaska the forty-ninth state. Alaska had its voice, and the American flag had a new star.

"NORTH TO THE FUTURE"

Since it became a state, Alaska has proved that Seward's instincts were right. Alaska is "worthy." As its motto promises, Alaska has brought the state and the country "north to the future." Its natural resources benefit both Alaska and the United States. One of the world's largest suppliers of seafood, Alaska harvests 2.5 million tons (2.3 million metric tons) a year, and its fishing industry contributes almost $1.1 billion a year to the state's economy.

Proud Alaskan fishermen display their catch of halibut.

Independence mine. Gold State Historical Park. Mining is a major source of revenue for Alaska.

Alaska's mining industry is also a major source of revenue and employment for the state. In 1993 the industry was valued at $500 million. In addition, the 128.9 million acres (52.2 million hectares) of forests, which cover 24 percent of Alaska's territory, provide the state with a thriving timber industry.

As profitable as all these resources are, Alaska's oil and natural gas deposits are the state's greatest natural assets. Approximately 85 percent of the money spent by the state government comes from oil and gas revenues. In 1968 when oil, or "black gold," was found in Prudhoe Bay on the Arctic Ocean, it was the richest oil field ever discovered in the United States.

Before this oil could be pumped out, an agreement had to be reached between the government and the Native Alaskans who lived in the area. The subject of Native Alaskan land

The Trans-Alaska Pipeline, which transports oil from Prudhoe Bay to the port of Valdez

rights could no longer be ignored. The time had come to answer the question, who exactly owned Alaska?

In 1971, Congress answered that question with the Alaska Native Claims Settlement Act, or ANCSA. ANCSA acknowledged that the native population had a right to a percentage of Alaska's land and a right to share in the state's financial future. Congress agreed to give various Native organizations 43.7 million acres (18 million hectares), or 11 percent of Alaska's territory. The remaining land was divided up among the federal government, the state government, and individuals.

Congress also agreed to pay Native Alaskans almost $1 billion. Over an eleven-year period, most of the money was deposited into twelve regional Native corporations. These corporations, such as the Arctic Slope Native Association and the Tlingit-Haida Central Council, used the funds to build Native Alaskan businesses.

Native Alaskans now had the right to self-determination, which is the right given all Americans to decide for them-selves what to do with their land and their money. They had the right to be part of Alaska's future—a future that included the development of Prudhoe Bay.

To transport the oil out of Prudhoe Bay, a group of eight oil corporations, called the Alyeska Pipeline Service Company, built the Trans-Alaska Pipeline. This 800-mile (1,285 km) long pipeline, which is 48 inches (1.2 meters) in diameter, runs south from Prudhoe Bay to the ice-free port of Valdez on the Gulf of Alaska. Worried that the pipeline would ruin the wilderness, **environmentalists**

★ ★ ★ ★

THE *EXXON VALDEZ* OIL SPILL

On March 24, 1989, the tanker *Exxon Valdez* ran aground, spilling eleven million gallons (42 million liters) of oil into Prince William Sound. A total of 250 million seabirds and thousands of sea animals were killed in this environmental disaster.

The clean up after the *Exxon Valdez* oil spill was hard and grueling work.

opposed its construction. Congress, however, approved the plan. The pipeline was completed in 1977 and cost $8 billion.

THE ARCTIC NATIONAL WILDLIFE REFUGE

Since the discovery of oil in Prudhoe Bay, there has been an ongoing debate regarding the further development of Alaska's oil and natural gas resources. In particular, there is great concern over whether or not to drill in the Arctic National Wildlife Refuge (ANWR). President Eisenhower established ANWR in 1960 as the country's last unspoiled region. In 1980 President Jimmy Carter doubled the size of the refuge. It now consists of 19.5 million acres (7.9 million hectares) where wildlife roam freely through the untouched Alaskan **tundra.**

The section of ANWR being considered for development is a 1.5-million-acre (0.6 million hectare) plain that lies between the Beaufort Sea to the north and the Brooks Mountain Range to the south. Many Alaskans who want the additional tax revenue for the state support oil exploration in this area. Many politicians believe that, regardless of one's position on conservation, the area must be drilled to end the country's dependence on imported oil from the Middle East. Finally, most who favor developing ANWR

A snowy owl is just one of the many forms of wildlife that inhabit the Arctic National Wildlife Refuge.

ALASKA'S PROTECTED LANDS

In the early 1900s the federal government began protecting portions of Alaska's wilderness. The first area set aside was the Tongass National Forest. Other protected areas include Chugach National Forest, Denali National Park, and Kenai Fjords National Park.

Caribou roam free in the Arctic Wildlife Refuge.

are confident that technology has advanced so far that the work can be done without harming the environment. As President George W. Bush has said, "We can do both—[take] out energy and [leave] only footprints."

Environmentalists disagree. They feel that the purity of the Alaskan wilderness must be preserved, especially in those places that were set aside for that purpose. They argue that the pipes, pumps, and buildings constructed for oil exploration will destroy the beauty of ANWR. They also believe that development of this plain will destroy the migration patterns of ANWR's wild animals.

Native Alaskans also are divided on what to do in ANWR. The Gwich'in people, who live south of the ANWR plain, worry that oil exploration will force the caribou they hunt for food to change their migration patterns and leave the area. They also fear that the development of the plain will destroy their cultural traditions, which are tied to the wilderness.

Evon Peter, a Gwich'in spokesman, has explained his people's position by saying, "The caribou for us are like the buffalo were to the Indians in the Lower 48." In addition, he sees the Gwich'in's "struggle" as "spiritual." To him it is "about dignity, respect, and the ways people relate to each other."

A bald eagle, the national bird of the United States, perches on a tree in Alaska.

George N. Ahnoagak, Sr., the mayor of the North Borough and an Inupiaq, believes otherwise. He has argued that development of the ANWR plain will not destroy the culture of the Native Alaskans who live there. Living near Prudhoe Bay, he has experienced a cooperation that worked. As he described it, "We have done battle with the oil industry and the government when they ignored our concerns. But, we have also seen the benefits of responsible oil extraction."

Finally, Ahnoagak also has argued that "Native people in the 21st century are not well-served by the attitude that indigenous cultures cannot survive unless their world remains untouched. . . . All healthy cultures continually adapt to changes in their environment."

Whatever the final decision on ANWR is, the conclusion reached will come out of the American democratic process. Politicians, businesspeople, writers, and ordinary citizens will discuss, argue, and ultimately vote until a resolution is found. It is the same process that brought Alaska from its beginnings as a vast Russian fur-trading station to the state it is today—not an icebox, not a joke, but a treasure filled with beauty, diversity, and a wealth of natural resources. Seward would be proud.

ALASKANS IN THE TWENTY-FIRST CENTURY

At the beginning of the new millennium, Alaska's population was approximately 619,500. A total of 75.2 percent were white, 16.4 percent Native Alaskan, 3.9 percent African American, and 4 percent Hispanic.

Glossary

canneries—factories for processing and canning fish

communist—a person who believes in communism, a political system in which the government, not individuals, controls the economy

delegate—a person who acts as a representative for another person or group

economy—the management of financial resources in a state or country

environmentalists—people who work to protect the natural world from destruction and pollution

folly—great error

indigenous—adjective that describes the original inhabitants of a place

infrastructure—the essential services needed to run a community, state, or country; such services include transportation, communications, water, and power lines

legislature—an officially elected group of people responsible for making laws

Lower 48—the term Alaskans use to describe the contiguous, or adjoining, forty-eight states to the south of Alaska

migrated—moved from one region to settle in another

natural resources—sources of wealth that occur in nature

nuggets—small chunks of rock or mineral

panhandle—a narrow strip of land jutting out from a larger, broader area

prospectors—people who explore a specific area for minerals such as gold

revenue—income produced from a specific source

tundra—a treeless area consisting of a permanently frozen subsoil in which plants such as lichen, mosses, and small shrubs grow

Timeline: Seward's

40,000–14,000 BCE	1741	1867	1884	1897	1912	1935
The first land migration of humans from northeast Asia into the North American landmass takes place.	The Russians arrive in Alaska	The United States buys Alaska from Russia for $7.2 million	The U.S. Congress passes the First Organic Act	The Klondike Gold Rush begins	The Second Organic Act passed	The Matanuska-Susitna Valley Project established

44

Folly

1942	1955	1959	1960	1968	1977	1989
The Japanese attack the Aleutian Islands in World War II	The Alaskan Constitutional Convention is held	Alaska becomes a state	The Arctic National Wildlife Refuge is (ANWR) established	Oil is discovered at Prudhoe Bay on the North Slope	The Trans-Alaska Pipeline completed	The *Exxon Valdez* oil spill

To Find Out More

BOOKS

Ferber, Edna. *Ice Palace.* Buccaneer Books, 1992.

Miller, Luree, and Scott Miller. *Alaska, Pioneer Stories of a Twentieth Century Frontier.* New York: Dutton, 1991.

Somervill, Barbara A. *Alaska.* Danbury, CT: Children's Press, 2002.

Tindall, George Brown, and David E. Shi. *America, a Narrative History, Vol. II.* New York: W.W. Norton, 1999.

Van Deusen, Glyndon G. *William Henry Seward.* New York: Oxford University Press, 1967.

ONLINE SITES

Alaskool
www.alaskool.org

ANWR
www.anwr.org

Everything Alaska
www.everythingalaska.com

Alaska Visitor Information
www.vacationalaska.com

Index

Bold numbers indicate illustrations.

Alaska National Wildlife Refuge, 38–39, **39,** 40–41, 45

Alaska Native Claims Settlement Act, 37

Alaskan Constitutional Convention, **30,** 31, 45

Alaska Purchase Treaty, 12, **13,** 14, 34, 44

Alaska Syndicate, 20, **20**

Ballinger-Pinchot affair, 22

Bering, Vitus, 10, **10**

Cannery, 20, 42

Committee of One Hundred, 29

communist, 26, 42

Delegate, 21–22, 42

Economy, 14, 27, 34, 37, 42

environmentalist, 37, 40, 42

Exxon Valdez, 38, **38,** 45

Farmland, **24,** 24–25, 44

First Organic Act, 16, 44

fur trade, 10, 19, 41

Gruening, Ernest, **28,** 29-33

Ice Palace, 33, **33**

indigenous, 8–9, 16, 27, 29, 35, 37, 40, 41, 42

infrastructure, 22-23, 27, 42

Klondike gold, **17,** 17–19, 44

Legislature, 22, 42

Lower 48, 7, 24, 40, 42

Migrate, 8, **8,** 42, 44

Natural resource, 4, 21, 23, 28, 31, 34, 35, 41, 42

nugget, 17, 18, 42

Panhandle, 16, 42

prospector, 17, 18, 42

Revenue, 4, 42

Second Organic Act, 22, 44

Seward, William, 10–11, **11,** 12, **13,** 16, 26, 32, 34

state flag, 33, **33,** 45

statehood, 16-17, 22, 27-28, **28,** 29-32, **32,** 33-34, 45

Territory, 7, 12, 16–17, 33

Trans-Alaska Pipeline, **36,** 37, 38, 45

tundra, 39, 42

Wickersham, James, **21,** 21–22, 28

About the Author

Melissa Whitcraft lives in Montclair, New Jersey, with her husband, their two sons, and their dog. She has a master of arts in theater. In addition to plays and poetry, she has written both fiction and nonfiction for children. She has published *Tales from One Street Over,* a chapter book for early elementary-grade readers. Her biography, *Francis Scott Key, a Gentleman of Maryland,* was published as a Franklin Watts First Book. Ms. Whitcraft has also written books on the Tigris and Euphrates, the Niagara, and the Hudson Rivers for the Watts Library series. She feels lucky to have experienced the wonders of Alaska firsthand.